An of

CW01506452

ACTIVE LONDON

Written by
ALICE PORTER

Design District Basketball Court (no.28)

INFORMATION IS DEAD.
LONG LIVE OPINION.

When we conceived these guidebooks, we feared they would fail. Who needs a guidebook when everything can be googled for free?

But then it occurred to us; that's exactly why you *do* want a guidebook. You want lively, trustworthy opinion combined with great photographs. You don't want endless information from a thousand online bots.

We think you are like us: you care about quality, you care about style, you care about provenance, but you don't have time to waste on long words like 'provenance'. You want to cut to the chase: where's good?

If you were to come and stay on our couch (it's a metaphor btw; we have a guide to hotels), these are the places we'd recommend.

Ann & Martin, co-founders
Hoxton Mini Press

MAD Mayfair (no.42)
Opposite: Richmond Cycling Loop (no.29)

Heartcore (no.43)
Opposite: London Grapple (no.34)

KEEP MOVING

It's easy to neglect moving your body in London. Sure, it's a non-stop city, but it's also designed for convenience, with transport options that mean you can avoid walking for even ten minutes if you don't want to. Most of our work lives involve sitting down for eight hours per day. Maybe you've tried your local chain gym, but found the strip lights and basement studios uninspiring, or discovered the trainers use toxic – and frankly annoying – phrases like 'bikini body'.

Let me assure you that exercise doesn't need to be a chore. And if there's a city that will present you with opportunities to find pleasure in movement, it's this one. While writing this book, I've discovered that Londoners find joy in moving their bodies in more ways than you could imagine – whether it's rolling around on the floor with strangers doing Jiu-Jitsu (no.34) or learning how to ballroom dance (no.1), cycling past deer in Richmond Park (no.29) or kayaking to a Hackney pub (no.13) instead of hopping on the bus. If the idea of spending 30 minutes on a cross trainer fills you with dread, you'll never have to again; here you will find an activity that gives you post-exercise endorphins you didn't believe existed.

Moving your body, particularly in a group setting, also requires a level of trust – signing up to a class where others are doing the same is an incredible way to connect. So many gyms, yoga studios and sports groups across London act as community hubs – and plenty of them are free or very affordable.

They're also some of the only places where the person standing next to you is up for a chat in between burpees or downward dogs. (Don't worry if you prefer to sweat in solitude; there are plenty of opportunities to exercise without small talk.)

Working out doesn't always have to be about pushing yourself to your limits or hitting a personal best; it can also be about having fun with others, experiencing the city in a different way, learning a new skill or relishing your own peace in the process. It's easy to take for granted the many ways in which we can move our bodies. You'll find as many options in this book for high-intensity cardio as there are for gentle, calm movement, as many ideas for outdoor adventures as indoor activities – and a multitude of solo pursuits alongside group sessions and sports.

Whether you're a die-hard wellness junkie who gets a kick out of Strava kudos, or a self-declared gym-phobe looking for a workout that finally clicks, this book will get you excited about exercise – and the prospect of doing it in London.

Alice Porter
London, 2025

Alice Porter is a south London-based writer with more active hobbies than she has time for. You'll often find her commuting straight from a weight lifting session to a zen yoga class – by bike, of course – and she's constantly surprised by how many sports she enjoys as an adult given her disdain for P.E. as a child.

BEST FOR...

Getting a sweat on

Sometimes it feels good to tire yourself out. Barry's Bootcamp (no.37) will leave you so exhausted, a full day on the couch afterwards is justified. Sweat by BXR's VersaClimbing workout (no.3) uses a machine that simulates climbing Everest, and leaves you with a similar sense of accomplishment.

Mindful movement

Gentle exercise benefits the mind as well as the body. You won't need much convincing of that after taking a yin yoga class at holistic wellness centre Seven Lion Yard (no.23), or visiting the beautiful Studio Anatomy (no.19) for a low-impact but challenging Reformer Pilates class.

Embracing the outdoors

London is the worst place to be an outdoorsy person, right? Not at Hampstead Heath, where you can immerse yourself in nature at the swimming ponds (no.48). If you prefer to be above the waterline, try stand-up paddleboarding in Richmond (no.31).

Helmet heads

If navigating inner-city cycling lanes fills you with mild terror, take a spin around Richmond Park (no.29), where you'll be dodging deer instead of double deckers. To learn how to track cycle, Herne Hill Velodrome (no.33) is a great day out.

Increasing your step count

Bored of stomping around your local park? Venture southeast to Sydenham Hill Wood (no.25) – one of London's oldest nature reserves – for a wander. For north Londoners, the Parkland Walk (no.51) starts in Finsbury Park and will guarantee just as much greenery and about the same number of steps.

Watching the wallet

For no-cost end-of-the-month endorphin highs, join run club Midnight Runners (no.2) for a bootcamp-style run around central London. Prefer something more relaxed? Terrible Football (no.52) offers free sessions across the city for people with little to no football experience, so is pain-free for your ego as well as your bank balance.

Trying something new

Push yourself out of your comfort zone with a beginner dance class at The Place (no.6). Looking for an even more unconventional way to spend your evening? Take a fencing lesson in central London (no.44), or head to Crystal Palace for a game of beach volleyball (no.26) – yes, even in winter.

Bringing out your competitive side

There's nothing wrong with some healthy competition. Put your serve to the test in London's famous tennis suburb at Wimbledon Park's public courts (no.30). Or try Padel in Canary Wharf (no.15), ideal for playing doubles. If racket sports don't rouse your inner athlete, Activate (no.35) is an active gaming experience that will set friend against friend.

1
SWING PATROL

Old-school partner dancing

Swing dancing is probably the quickest way to impress your mates at a wedding and it's also a joyful, sociable way to move your body. Swing Patrol hosts weekly classes across various church halls in the city, frequented by nervous first-timers who aren't sure exactly what they've signed up for. The style of dance is called the Lindy Hop and it's the kind of swinging partner dancing you see in old movies. Every class starts with learning the basic steps, then you'll decide if you want to lead or follow and then pair up. There's always one person who thinks they're auditioning for *Strictly*, but most are happy to chat mid-dance and giggle when you inevitably mess up your steps.

Various locations, check online for details
swingpatrol.co.uk

2

MIDNIGHT RUNNERS

Electric group runs

Running is an incredible way to get an endorphin boost. But holding yourself accountable when it comes to putting your trainers on and heading out can be tough. That's why run clubs exist, and Midnight Runners is one of London's most popular. They hold regular events that will help you stick to your training goals, including bootcamp-style runs, which stop every few kilometres to complete strength and conditioning exercises (or just take a breather). There are also party runs around events like Halloween and rave runs that feature DJ sets and light shows, which are fairly relaxed if you want a walking break. All runs are volunteer-led and free to join, with sessions at least twice a week.

Various locations, check online for details
midnightrunners.com

3

SWEAT BY BXR

Elite-level training with state-of-the-art equipment

Think you've tried every form of cardio? Let us introduce the VersaClimber, a machine that mimics the natural motion of climbing. Stand on the steps of the vertical climber, a bit like a cross trainer, and hold on to the handles above your head, moving your legs and arms up and down simultaneously. It feels a bit silly, but it's a seriously effective workout, hitting the sweet spot between low-impact and high-intensity. The gym, which also offers boxing, yoga and Pilates, is located on the 25th floor, with impressive views that help distract from your own breathlessness and the instructor's motivational cues – 'pain is temporary' or 'you're stronger than you think' – which can either inspire or infuriate, depending on your mood.

22 Bishopsgate, EC2N 4BQ
Nearest stations: Bank, Liverpool Street
sweatbybxr.com

4

PINEAPPLE DANCE STUDIOS

A London institution for dancers of all levels

If you have ever fantasised about being on stage, you owe it to yourself to take a class at this iconic dance studio. The studio spans four floors, with narrow corridors lined by women in leotards stretching. It's not unusual to spot West End performers training here, but plenty of the 100+ weekly classes are tailored to beginners. There really is something for everyone, whether you dreamt of being a backing dancer or the star of *Chicago*. Beginner classes follow a straightforward format: 15 minutes warming up, then learning some simple choreography, with lots of options to make it easier and teachers who are enthusiastic and engaging.

7 Langley Street, WC2H 9JA
Nearest station: Covent Garden
pineapple.uk.com

5

FRAME

Joyful fitness classes

For those nostalgic for '80s fitness classes, leg warmers and all, Frame is a studio focused on having fun, whether you're bouncing on a mini trampoline or channelling Cher in step aerobics. Although they cover all the traditional workouts like yoga and Pilates, this is the perfect place to step out of your comfort zone. Try Dance Cardio – like Zumba, but with better choreography and nostalgic, guilty-pleasure pop music. Or live out your teenage pop star fantasies in the Music Video class, where you'll learn Britney-esque noughties choreography (hair whipping is a given). Neither instructors nor attendees put too much focus on getting the moves precisely right, so be ready to embrace silliness.

29 New Inn Yard, EC2A 3EY
Nearest station: Shoreditch High Street
moveyourframe.com

6

THE PLACE

Nurturing, creative dance classes

Learning to dance feels like a truly creative act at The Place. While some students train here full time, evening classes and summer schools are available for beginners. Choose from ballet, contemporary and niche styles like Tanztheater (German Expressionist dance). You can drop into a class at any point during term, but most people sign up for a 12-week course. Participants vary widely in experience, from novices to ex-pros brushing up on their skills, and dancers 50 years apart in age regularly share the floor. As well as learning choreography and technique, exercises are designed to spark creativity and include some improv. Instructors take their craft seriously, so lean into your inner drama kid to get the most out of the classes.

17 Duke's Road, WC1H 9PY
Nearest station: Euston
theplace.org.uk

7

THE NEW RIVER PATH

Find nature north of the river

If anyone ever claims that north London isn't green, take them along the New River Path. Confusingly, this isn't a river; it's an aqueduct. Nor is it particularly new, having been built in 1613 to bring drinking water to the region. But you'd be forgiven for calling a stream an ocean when you've spent too long in the city, and this walk can feel like an oasis amid the claustrophobic high rises. The London part of the route takes you through Clissold Park – known for its wildlife and for very good sandwiches at Finks Pump House – and Walthamstow Wetlands nature reserve, finishing at Alexandra Palace. Overall, it's an impressive 11.4 km with plenty of foodie spots to refuel a short detour along the way.

New River Head, 173 Rosebery Avenue, EC1R 4TY
Nearest station: Angel

8

GOODGYM

Genuinely rewarding exercise

If running on a treadmill or completing hundreds of sit-ups feels pointless, this community fitness initiative will provide some real workout motivation. GoodGym is a non-profit founded to tackle the loneliness epidemic and build community. They host regular meetups that incorporate exercise into completing good deeds. Weekly sessions are led by trainers and involve running or cycling to a particular location to take part in a community initiative. You can also sign up for one-off tasks like an hour of gardening or delivering hot meals to those in need. It's free to sign up, although you're encouraged to make a small donation – which is a lot cheaper than a gym membership and provides far more incentive to exercise.

Various locations, check website for details
goodgym.org

9

EPPING FOREST CHESTNUT TRAIL

An enchanting way to get your steps in

You might not know it as anything more than the final destination on the Central line, but Epping is home to an 8,000-acre forest, making it the ideal playground for a weekend adventure walk. The Chestnut Trail is just over 5 km long and mostly flat along forest paths, so even at a ponderous pace it shouldn't take more than two hours. You'll clock up around 7,000 steps, so will easily hit your daily 10,000 target with the walk to and from the station. The best times to visit are October and May, depending on whether you prefer blazing copper leaves or budding spring greenery. Either way, you'll find yourself checking Citymapper to make sure you're really only 25 minutes from Liverpool Street.

Warren Road, Wanstead Park, E11 2LS
Nearest station: Wanstead

10

JUBILEE GREENWAY

Lush urban walking route

Created for the Queen's Diamond Jubilee, this sur-prisingly verdant walk covers a kilometre for each year Elizabeth II spent on the throne. At 60 km long, you can commit to a serious exploration of the city or, if you'd prefer not to tackle an ultra-marathon on a Sunday, opt to walk just part of it. Avoid crowds taking selfies at Buckingham Palace and throngs of preteen goths in Camden – start instead at Victoria Park, heading southeast past London Stadium towards the river (sections 3 and 4). You can wrap it up there with 13.7 km under your belt. For competitive step-counters, continue to Greenwich (section 5) and you'll have completed a half marathon, ideally timing it with a sunset view from the Royal Observatory.

St Mark's Gate, E9 5HT
Nearest station: Hackney Wick
tfl.gov.uk/modes/walking/jubilee-greenway

11

THE LINE

An artsy walk along the river

Looking for a fun way to reach 10,000 steps? This 7.2 km route should almost precisely hit it and you'll see several pieces of art along the way. Ideal for urbanites who prefer cityscapes to landscapes, it's London's only public art trail. Starting at Stratford's Olympic Park, you'll see sculptures by artists like Anish Kapoor, Madge Gill and Antony Gormley – including a precariously placed pylon that might cause alarm if you didn't know it was art. You can walk the whole thing or take the DLR for part of the route. A detailed map is available online and worth keeping handy, as the trail can feel more like an art hunt than a straightforward path. Avoid too many wrong turns and it should take around two hours.

9 Endeavour Square, E20 1JN
Nearest station: Stratford
the-line.org

12

LONDON FIELDS LIDO

Heated pool in the heart of Hackney

This Olympic-sized pool is a much-loved Hackney hangout, whether you want to train like a pro or just catch-up with your mates mid-doggy paddle. Divided into sections based on how seriously you take your swim, there are separate lanes for leisurely lengths as well as for those who want to put their goggles on and get their heads down – it's a popular spot for triathletes in training. There's a sun deck for lounging on hot days, though you'll be glad to know that this is one of the few city lidos that's heated all year round, so no gritting your teeth and pretending you like cold water swimming. Go at the weekend and grab lunch at Broadway Market, just through the park, when the post-swim hunger hits.

London Fields West Side, E8 3EU
Nearest station: London Fields
better.org.uk

13

MOO CANOES

Fun and fitness on London's waterways

Paddling along the River Lea is excellent for two reasons: a full upper-body workout and endless people watching. Moo's eye-catching cow-print canoes are suitable for up to three people, making them perfect for a catch-up with your mates, and tandem kayaks are also available. This is a fun way to explore Hackney Marshes, which feel surprisingly rural, or head towards the Olympic Park for a great view of the iconic stadium from the water. This is also a good point to park your kayak and grab lunch or a drink at Grow, an artsy, eco-friendly spot serving seasonal Middle Eastern food and natural wines.

The Milk Float Barge Sweetwater Moorings, E9 5EN
Nearest station: Hackney Wick
moocanoes.com

14

OVERGRAVITY GYMNASTICS

Learn to jump, flip and fly

Always dreamed of being able to casually backflip or drop into the splits as your party trick, despite having never really mastered a cartwheel? It's not too late to live out your gymnast dreams – at least not at OverGravity, who offer workshops on everything from simple tumbling to advanced acrobatics. The venue feels nostalgic, filled with bright blue and red mats like the childhood gymnasiums you might remember. Plenty of people who have never even attempted a handstand turn up to beginner classes, so you won't be alone if you're nervous. Instructors walk you through everything, with equal priority given to safety as well as pushing you out of your comfort zone. You'll progress in no time.

Arches 160–163 Sutton Street, E1 0DB
Nearest station: Shadwell
overgravitygymnastics.uk

15
PADIUM

Padel courts designed for socialising

Padel is the latest craze in racket sports, and you'll be glad to know it's a lot easier to pick up than its slightly snooty cousin, tennis. It follows the same principles but with smaller courts, a harder, more compact racket and underarm serves – and is generally played in doubles, making it more social. Padium is well set up for that, with plenty of sofas and table tennis on its mezzanine level, plus seven indoor and two outdoor courts. You'll need to bring your own balls, but can hire rackets for a fiver. There's an on-site shop stocked with fancy equipment if you decide you want to get serious about Padel, as well as kit from premium brands like Babolat and Wilson.

10 Bank Street, E14 4DE
Nearest station: Canary Wharf
padium.com

16

LONDON AQUATICS CENTRE

Dive into an architectural masterpiece

You may have spotted this swimming centre, notable for its striking wave-like roof, when wandering around Stratford. If not, you'll probably remember it from the 2012 Olympics, for which it was custom-built by Zaha Hadid Architects. It's a must-visit for hydrophiles looking for a step up from their local leisure centres. There are three pools, two of which are Olympic-sized; the third is a diving pool with boards up to ten metres high. Walk in Tom Daley's footsteps and try your hand at diving with a beginner session, or buy a one-off swim for less than a tenner and stick to doing lengths. With panoramic windows and ceilings that undulate through the building, it's the best view you'll ever have during backstroke.

Queen Elizabeth Olympic Park, E20 2ZQ
Nearest station: Stratford
londonaquaticscentre.org

17

EAST OF EDEN

Walthamstow's wellness wonderland

There's no intimidation or cliquiness at this community fitness studio – in fact, it's one of the most welcoming wellness spots in the city. Decked out with soft greenery, the studio enjoys tonnes of natural light, and the founder Abby genuinely cares about fostering an inclusive space for movement. Over 200 classes are on offer, including Reformer Pilates, spin and hot yoga, plus great pre- and post-natal options. With excellent guidance from friendly instructors in all classes, it's really just a case of choosing which one you think you'd enjoy the most. Or better yet, plan your very own wellness day by attending a few and finish off with a healthy lunch at their Insta-friendly cafe.

Studio 1, 14 Hatherley Mews, E17 4QP
Nearest station: Walthamstow Central
eastofeden.uk

18
STRONGHOLD

Between a rock and a soft place

Bouldering can have an iffy reputation as a mid-life crisis hobby for millennial men, but the crowd here is more diverse and friendlier than you'd imagine. Granted, there will be some people dramatically rolling backwards off the wall, but most can be found sitting on the mats, chatting while awaiting their turn. Book an hour-long induction, where an instructor will warm you up and take you through the beginner climbs in a small group. You'll build strength quickly, even if you're new to exercise. Buy a day pass and you can take it at your own pace, with as many breaks as you'd like. And don't worry about falling – it's not common, but if your grip does slip, the floors are well cushioned with thick mats.

Unit 30, Canal Place, Andrews Road, E8 4FX
Nearest station: Cambridge Heath
Other location: Tottenham Hale
thestrongholduk.com

19

STUDIO ANATOMY

A Reformer Pilates studio with aesthetic appeal

If you're put off gyms because of their sterile layouts, strip lighting and bored staff, you'll be delighted with Studio Anatomy, which is the antithesis of this. It's split across two floors, the first being home to their Reformer Pilates studio, which uses sliding carriages with adjustable springs to develop strength and mobility. Upstairs you'll find functional fitness classes featuring strengthening exercises combined with bodyweight cardio and an infrared sauna for post-workout recuperation. Instructors are thorough, particularly in beginner classes, so you won't feel lost if this is your first time. This doesn't mean the classes aren't challenging, but the bright and airy space is somewhere you'll always look forward to visiting – no matter how much discomfort you put your muscles through.

1 King Edward's Road, E9 7SF
Nearest station: London Fields
studioanatomy.co.uk

20

CALI KULTURE

Build bodyweight strength

If you've only ever seen calisthenics in its most difficult form – people defying gravity by balancing their entire body weight in a contorted handstand – you might have assumed it's not for you. But just as you wouldn't start running by attempting a marathon, you don't need to be able to do one-handed pull-ups to try calisthenics. Cali Kulture's beginner classes only entry requirement is to be able to hang from a bar for ten seconds. In the hour-long class, you'll practise pull-ups, push-ups and dips, with plenty of modifications available. It's one of the best upper-body and core workouts around, guided by supportive instructors. Classes are held at three London gyms – mainly Mission, a bougie studio with a sauna and Bramley products in the showers.

7–9 Fashion Street, E1 6PX
Nearest stations: Aldgate East, Liverpool Street
Other locations: London Fields, Walthamstow
cali-kulture.com

21

BASIC SPACE

Stripped-back yoga classes in south London

With so many swanky studios around, it's easy to forget that all you really need to practise yoga is a mat and a quiet room. This south London studio is proof of that. The name references the simple space, though it is well-designed with inviting, Scandi-inspired interiors. Their yoga classes are some of the best in the city, with excellent teachers choreographing creative and nurturing flows. Whether it's an active practice to feel the burn or restorative poses for the best stretch you've had in years, the priority is good-quality movement. There's a range of other classes on offer too, including prenatal yoga, Pilates and barre. It's well worth taking an afternoon to try one out and signing up as a member if you're local.

Unit 4, Camberwell Passage, SE5 0AX
Nearest station: Denmark Hill
Other location: Stockwell
basicspacelondon.com

22
NUE GROUND

If heaven were a wellness studio

You know the version of yourself you imagine when you've woken early, exercised and written an ambitious to-do list? That's who you'll be at Nue Ground. This small fitness studio feels luxe thanks to the neutral decor and branded equipment. The classes range from restorative yoga, where you'll be encouraged to spend as much time as possible in child's pose, to Pilates and barre, with instructors who provide strict direction that makes you feel a bit like a kid at ballet class. The cafe is a plant-filled paradise that could trick you into thinking you've crossed a threshold between Clapham and Bali. If the weather permits it, enjoy a matcha moment after class in the sun-drenched outdoor seating area.

32 Abbeville Road, SW4 9NG
Nearest station: Clapham South
nueground.co.uk

23

SEVEN LION YARD

A healing space for yoga and meditation

You don't have to drip with sweat or ache for days to benefit from moving your body. In fact, gentle movement that prioritises mental health as much as physical fitness can be transformative. That's the mantra at Seven Lion Yard, a wellbeing centre that provides holistic therapies as well as meditation and yoga. The group mindfulness practices take place in the loft – which enjoys tonnes of natural light during the day – and there are candlelit classes in the evenings. Offerings include yin yoga, which involves holding five or six poses for a prolonged period, and sound baths, where instructors use bowls, gongs and chimes to relax you during meditation. There's usually no more than ten to a class, and the idea is to engage in peaceful contemplation.

7 Lion Yard, Tremadoc Road, SW4 7NQ
Nearest stations: Clapham High Street, Clapham North
sevenlionyard.com

24
GREENWICH PENINSULA GOLF RANGE

Practise your swing with a pint

Always fancied yourself someone who spends weekends on the golf course? This is the closest you'll get in the city, but it's a good urban alternative. With panoramic views of London, this driving range is the perfect sunset spot. Don't panic if your only experience of golf is Wii Sports; booking a bay here is more about socialising than training. Each bay includes a sofa and table for ordering food and drinks – but the costs here can add up quickly once you factor in renting balls and a club, too. Instead, work up an appetite while playing and then head south, away from the O2 with its chains, and visit the cosy Pelton Arms for delicious pizza.

265 Tunnel Avenue, SE10 0QE
Nearest station: North Greenwich
greenwichpeninsulagolfrange.com

25
SYDENHAM HILL WOOD

Reset with a walk in ancient woodland

One of the best things about London is all the newness, but if you're feeling overwhelmed trying to keep up with the latest restaurant openings and must-see exhibitions, take a stroll in the ancient Sydenham Hill Wood. You'll pass through age-old groves, with trees that were once reserved by Elizabeth I for shipbuilding but thankfully remain in what is one of south London's greenest spaces. It's hard to believe you're just 8 km from Big Ben as you wander through fields of bluebells, spotting frogs and newts. Your only reminder that the city is still spinning is the view of the BT Tower and the Houses of Parliament across Dulwich College, which marks the end of the walk.

Crescent Wood Road, SE26 6LS
Nearest station: Sydenham Hill

26

DEEP DISH VOLLEYBALL

Serving up an urban beach

You don't need to be on a far-flung tropical beach to enjoy a game of volleyball; these urban beach volleyball courts are open year-round, whatever the weather. It might not be the Caribbean, but when you lock into the game, you'll forget the concrete surrounds of the local sports centre. This is a sport that brings out everyone's competitive edge, plus you'll get a full-body workout. Either hire a court with three friends for as little as £20 an hour, or sign up to a class or social group, plenty of which are catered to beginners. You'll almost definitely find yourself in fits of laughter as you take an inevitably dramatic fall (don't worry, sand provides a comfy cushion).

Crystal Palace National Sports Centre, SE19 2BB
Nearest station: Crystal Palace
deepdishbeach.com/crystal-palace

27

BEND IT LIKE PECKHAM

Unleash your inner Lioness

If you're put off playing football because of its lad culture, this south London grassroots football club might convert you. Their trans-inclusive women's and non-binary team sessions feel like a fun kickabout with your mates, plus some coaching. The two-hour weekly meets start with a warm-up, some simple drills and then a game: either five-, seven- or eleven-a-side, depending on how many turn up. You don't need any fancy kit, although football boots are recommended in winter. Sessions only cost a few pounds and you can go as little or often as you'd like (there's no pressure to sign up for a season). They meet on Peckham Rye Common every Saturday at 11am, followed by chips at the pub.

Peckham Rye Common, SE15 3UA
Nearest station: Peckham Rye
instagram.com/benditlikepeckham_se15

28

DESIGN DISTRICT BASKETBALL COURT

Hoops with a view

Struggling to find a way to get together with your mates that isn't just... pub? Why not hire this rooftop basketball court and enjoy a slam-dunk afternoon on the Greenwich Peninsula for the price of approximately four central London pints. You'll generally play five-a-side and, depending on how experienced and/or competitive you are, you can take the rules seriously or make up your own as you'll have the court to yourself. Unequalled panoramic views of the Canary Wharf skyline mean there's plenty to take in, even if you get demoted to the bench.

Floor 3, Building c1, Cripps Yard,
Soames Walk, se10 0bq
Nearest station: North Greenwich
designdistrict.co.uk/whats-here/basketball-court

29

RICHMOND CYCLING LOOP

A rural mecca for city cyclists

Taking a spin around Richmond Park is practically a rite of passage as a London cyclist. It also offers welcome respite from the things that make cycling in London tedious: traffic, roadworks and angry bus drivers stuck behind you. The route around this glorious parkland is nearly 11 km and it's well populated with fellow cyclists, pedestrians and, if you keep an eye out, wild deer. Start at Roehampton Gate and go anticlockwise, doing a few loops if you have the time. Cars are allowed on parts of the route, so it's best to go early: turn up when the gates open at around 7am and you'll get to experience pure cycling joy in one of the most peaceful parts of London.

Roehampton Gate, Richmond Park, SW15 5JY
Nearest station: Barnes

30

WIMBLEDON PARK TENNIS COURTS

The perfect excuse to don your tennis whites

If you're even slightly interested in tennis and the tournament that takes place in this London suburb each year, visit Wimbledon Park for a hit. The 20 courts are tiered uphill with the overground running above, which makes for a great Insta opportunity from the dedicated viewing point. Booking online is a breeze, and you can choose from hard courts – painted purple and green in homage to the All England Club – or well-maintained Astroturf. Although some of the best players in the world are just around the corner, these are public courts, so no one will expect your backhand to resemble Emma Raducanu's. You're as likely to swap balls with young families as you are players in full kit taking their serve seriously.

Home Park Road, SW19 7HR
Nearest station: Wimbledon Park
clubspark.lta.org.uk/wimbledonpark

31

PADDLE RICHMOND

Stand-up paddleboarding adventures

Once you've mastered the art of not falling in, stand-up paddleboarding is easier than it looks – and it'll build better core strength than sit-ups ever could. It's easy to forget it's a workout at all, as you paddle down the banks of the enchanting Richmond riverside. You can hire a board, or book a lesson or tour if you want guidance and the opportunity to spot wildlife. If you're not fussed by kingfishers or early-morning otter sightings, time your session with high tide, so you can oar your way to The White Cross – better known as 'the pub that floods'. The beer garden can flood up to 4.5 metres, so you might get soggy ankles with your fish and chips.

Richmond Bridge Boathouses,
Richmond Riverside, TW9 1TH
Nearest station: Richmond
paddlerichmond.co.uk

32

BATTERSEA PARK TO GREENWICH CYCLE ROUTE

Scenic riverside ride with plenty of pit stops

Ever wondered whether it might actually be quicker to walk between southwest and southeast London than to take public transport? You'll get there on two wheels with far less hassle. The cycle between Battersea Park and Greenwich is almost completely riverside, which means minimal checks of your sat nav and no angry horns from cabbies. You'll feel confident on this route even if you're more used to Lime than road bikes. It's 16 km, which should take about an hour, but you'll pass plenty of iconic landmarks around the South Bank and Canary Wharf – the perfect excuse for a break. Make a pit stop at Greenwich Market and carb-load on street food before the journey back.

Albert Bridge, SW11 4PL
Nearest station: Battersea Park

33

HERNE HILL VELODROME

An Olympic-style cycling experience

If you've always fancied yourself a track cyclist and are looking for an opportunity to don your obnoxiously big cycling sunnies, this is the place to do it. The sport isn't reserved for Olympians and triathletes – at least not at Herne Hill Velodrome. It hosted the Olympics back in 1948, but this two-wheeling south London institution puts community first. So, despite the inevitable crowd of Lycra-clad cyclists pushing for 60 km per hour, you'll feel at ease even if your stabilisers have just been taken off (and they offer lessons for both kids and adults). Take part in taster sessions, and if it rouses your competitive side, you can work towards a training accreditation so you can participate in races.

104 Burbage Road, SE24 9HE
Nearest station: Herne Hill
hernehillvelodrome.com

34

LONDON GRAPPLE

Fight the good fight

Smiling while in a headlock? You're probably at this Brazilian Jiu-Jitsu gym in Deptford. This marital art emphasises technique over strength, meaning height and sex are irrelevant. To an untrained eye, it might look like people rolling around on the floor, but they're using specific techniques. You can learn these at Grapple's introductory class on Thursdays at 6pm. It's designed for beginners, but plenty of seasoned members attend, so you'll be paired with someone who knows what they're doing and will kindly guide you. Don't be nervous if you've never tried martial arts before: despite the fact that participants can easily put you in a chokehold, this is one of the friendliest gyms in London.

Unit 1, Ffinch Street, SE8 5QA
Nearest station: Deptford
londongrapple.co.uk

35

ACTIVATE AT THE O2

Fitness meets fun with action-packed IRL gaming

Remember when you were a kid and moving your body was fun and playful? This immersive gaming experience will help you rediscover that feeling. Go with a group of mates, between three and five players, and spend an adrenaline-filled hour switching between nine interactive game rooms. Dynamic puzzles and challenges use clever technology that responds in real time to your movements, such as Mega Grid, where you'll test your reflexes jumping and running between 500 LED floor squares, and a *Squid Game*-like challenge where you'll hide from a huge, illuminated eye while completing tasks. Even those who claim to be non-competitive will be wildly invested – and you'll break a serious sweat, no matter your fitness level.

Peninsula Square, SE10 0DX
Nearest station: North Greenwich
playactivate.co.uk

36

ROWBOTS

A heart-thumping rowing machine workout

Still looking for a way to do cardio that doesn't make you feel like gouging your eyes out? Rowbots is a fitness studio for the running-averse, offering full-body workouts for rowing rookies and seasoned pros alike. The 50-minute classes involve sprints on a rowing machine followed by floor-based strength training, like dumbbell squats and burpees. The studio is dark, the beats are loud and the high-intensity workouts are steered by equally high-energy trainers with impressive qualifications – and you'll truly benefit from their advice thanks to the small class sizes. You can set your own pace and spend as much time as you like in the fancy waterfall showers afterwards, which will be necessary after an epically sweaty session.

6 Great Titchfield Street, W1W 8BB
Nearest station: Oxford Circus
rowbots.co.uk

37

BARRY'S BOOTCAMP

HIIT for workout warriors

Want a Saturday morning gym session with the same energy as a Friday night out? Head to Barry's for a clubby vibe, music loud enough to make the floors throb and like-minded grinders shamelessly sweating. You'll be running intervals in between dumbbell exercises, fuelled by endorphins rather than shots of baby Guinness, in the Red Room – which sounds very *Fifty Shades* but simply refers to the club-inspired lighting. Instructors are mic'd up, '90s boy band style, so they can announce what speed you should set your treadmill to, but you won't be alone if you opt for something slower. The coaches mainly act as hype men and also have a knack for curating euphoric playlists.

59 Kingly Street, W1B 5QL
Nearest station: Oxford Circus
Other locations: multiple, see website
barrys.com

HUSTLE
& HEART
— ◆ —
WILL SET YOU APART
Made in Canary Wharf

38

JAB BOXING

Bougie boxing classes

If your idea of a boxing gym is smelly gloves and grunting geezers, you'll be pleasantly surprised by JAB. This is one of London's fanciest gyms, with a recovery studio that boasts an ice bath *and* a sauna, luxurious changing rooms and a velvet-clad seating area with a juice bar. As well as feeling suitably swanky, you'll also get a top-notch work-out. Classes involve 30 minutes of swinging at a punchbag followed by 20 minutes of HIIT, with strength classes on offer, too. Those who train here are seriously fit, but you don't have to be: the lights are lowered, so you have the freedom to follow the coach's instructions or simply do your own thing and let off some steam.

Unit 5, Colonnade Walk,
151 Buckingham Palace Road, SW1W 9SZ
Nearest station: Victoria
jabboxing.club

39

REBASE

A recovery studio for ultimate rejuvenation

It's hard to say whether this wellness wonderland feels more like a glimpse into the past or the future. On the one hand, the marble ice baths on the underground level make you feel a bit like you're in ancient Rome. But then there's also a hyperbaric oxygen chamber and cryotherapy on offer, which is a sure reminder that you're living in the time of Google rather than gladiators. The aim of the game at Rebase is recovery, both muscular and mental. As well as infrared saunas, lymphatic drainage and IV vitamin infusions, there are also group and one-to-one yoga sessions on offer, ensuring a full-spectrum package of TLC for weary bodies and souls.

1a St Vincent Street, W1U 4DA
Nearest station: Bond Street
rebaserecovery.com

40

7BREATHS

Calm amid the chaos of central London

Nothing quite triggers the body's stress response like walking down Oxford Street – so find your zen in this tranquil meditation studio, just around the corner. Excellent sound-proofing means the only reminder of your location is that half the attendees are lying on their mats in smart business attire. There is a gong, but any heavy spirituality stops there. You won't feel intimidated if this is your first time trying meditation and instructors will pay no mind if you choose to spend the 45 minutes napping rather than doing guided breathwork or gentle stretches. With pillows, blankets and eye masks available, it can be difficult to resist the urge to nod off...

4 Rathbone Square, W1T 1EB
Nearest station: Tottenham Court Road
7breathsmeditation.com

41

BARRECORE

Unique blend of ballet, yoga and Pilates

Deterred by Barre at the thought of tutus and classical music? Don't write it off yet. Drawing from the rigorous training of ballet rather than its performance, sessions at Barrecore will help you achieve a ballerina's strength and posture – without any risk of stage fright. The focus is on precise, high-quality movement to improve muscular endurance, incorporating light weights and isometric contractions – tiny, controlled pulses that target the arms, legs and core, making the muscles tremble. Barrecore is home to an unpretentious crowd who are there for a properly good workout, aided by skilled instructors ready to help with hands-on adjustments. Bonus points for the bougie showers, where you can douse yourself in Cowshed products after class.

372 King's Road, SW3 5UZ
Nearest stations: Fulham Broadway, Imperial Wharf
Other locations: multiple, see website
barrecore.com

42

MAD MAYFAIR

Reformer Pilates on steroids

If you're the kind of person who gets a thrill from a full-body burn, you should try Lagree. It's similar to Reformer Pilates – using equipment with moving platforms and adjustable springs to provide resistance – although don't let anyone at Lagree studio MAD hear you say that (the first thing you'll see at the entrance is a neon sign that reads, 'It's not Pilates, it's Lagree'). You'll work out on a machine called a Megaformer; the focus is on time under tension, moving your muscles through planks and lunges as slowly as possible, which leaves you sore for days but promises quick results. The studio is nestled between Michelin star restaurants, so don't be surprised to spot a celebrity squatting next to you.

32 North Audley Street, W1K 6ZG
Nearest station: Marble Arch
Other location: Chelsea
letsgomad.com

43

HEARTCORE

Mindful Pilates

If you find yoga too spiritual and Pilates too clinical, this hybrid workout concept might hit the sweet spot. It takes place on a Pilates Reformer – a sliding bed controlled by straps and ropes – with exercises focusing on both mindfulness and muscle burn. You'll likely start with sun salutations and popular yoga-inspired poses, as well as Pilates-style holds and pulses that will leave you sore for days. Newbies receive individual tuition in using the Reformer and the instructors correct your form discreetly, slipping their mics off so you don't feel like you're being called out. The eight studios are decorated with colourful prints and plants, which feels deceptively cosy given how tough the workouts are.

57 Ossington Street, W2 4LY
Nearest stations: Bayswater, Notting Hill Gate
Other locations: multiple, see website
weareheartcore.com

44

CENTRAL LONDON FENCING CLUB

Channel your inner musketeer

Looking for a more engaging workout than endless burpees and crunches? Try a taster session at this club, where you can fantasise that you're part of a high-stakes Shakespearean duel. Fencing, often described as 'physical chess', requires as much mental energy as it does physical, combining strategy with strength-building moves like lunges and squats. It will also get your heart rate up, because you're constantly moving. Beginner classes are two hours long, covering the basics, with warm-ups, footwork drills and partner practice using an épée (the technical name for what everyone calls a sword).

98 Regency Street, SW1P 4GH
Nearest station: Pimlico
centrallondonfencingclub.co.uk

45

ROSS NYE STABLES

Canter through the royal park

Ever feel a pang of envy when you see someone galloping through the park on a perfect sunny day? There's no reason you can't put yourself in the saddle. Get started at Ross Nye Stables, which offers private and group rides, and you'll enjoy the scenic route through Hyde Park – even if trying to control the horse feels equal parts baffling and terrifying initially. Guided lessons include help mounting and dismounting, so you can focus on the views and bracing your core. Although you'll be sitting down, this is a surprisingly good workout, engaging core strength and a wide range of muscles – particularly if you're nervously clenching them.

8 Bathurst Mews, W2 2SB
Nearest station: Lancaster Gate
rossnyestables.co.uk

46

PADDINGTON RECREATION GROUND

Race around the track

There's something about running on a track that makes you go that little bit faster. At Paddington rec, the 400-metre track is free to use and is an ideal location for improving your pace or setting a PB. If you like to run in a group, run clubs like Track Mafia (Thursdays at 6:30pm) and Serpentine Run Club (Mondays at 7pm) offer free training sessions here. Around the track is calisthenics equipment that's available to the public – and plenty of it, so you won't queue for your preferred piece of kit. There are also football and hockey pitches and tennis and basketball courts – enough to keep you entertained all weekend (you could even plan your very own Olympics).

Randolph Avenue, W9 1PF
Nearest station: Maida Vale

47
WALK THE THAMES

Stroll through history along the iconic riverside

Walking riverside is one of the best ways to take in the city while hitting your step count. The Thames Path – 298 km long in total – isn't doable in a day, even for those who wear their pedometers as a badge of honour. It starts in the Cotswolds and ends in Woolwich, but nearly 130 km pass through London, with plenty of ways to split that up into a walk long enough to earn you kudos on Strava and short enough that you're in the pub by 5pm. Start west at Richmond Riverside, walking along the south bank and cheering on rowers as you cross Hammersmith Bridge, or begin at Chelsea Embankment, cross over Westminster Bridge and finish at Tower Bridge: each should take around 2–3 hours.

TW9 1EP to SW13 9EA
or SW3 5HH to SE1 2UP
Nearest stations: Richmond, Sloane Square
walkthethames.co.uk

48

HAMPSTEAD HEATH SWIMMING PONDS

A beloved oasis for all-level swimmers

It's hard to find a better spot in London for wild swimming than Hampstead Heath. The three ponds – mixed, men's and women's – offer a restorative plunge into nature, where the (admittedly brackish) waters are surrounded by what feels like endless greenery and you'll likely share your lane with a mallard or five. The mixed pond is just over 300 metres long, so you'll certainly get a good workout by doing a few lengths. And the post-dip endorphins feel especially satisfying when they hit during a slightly soggy walk in one of London's most beautiful parks, on your way to find a sweet treat (the pistachio doughnuts at the nearby Karma Bread bakery will satisfy sugar cravings).

Hampstead Heath, NW5 1QR
Nearest stations: Hampstead Heath, Gospel Oak
hampsteadheath.net

49
LEA VALLEY WALK

Trek along the towpath

Level up your weekend canal-side stroll with this near-25 km walk along the Lea Valley towpath. It starts in Waltham Cross – only 20 minutes from Liverpool Street – and ends at the East India Docks. With no breaks, it should take about five hours, but we suggest stopping halfway for a pint and pizza at Crate Brewery. If you don't care about your step count enough to spend the whole day walking, just do the fourth part of the route. A respectable 5.3 km, it begins at Clapton station and takes you through some of the walk's best bits, including Hackney Henge – east London's take on the stone circle – and Hackney Marshes. With 88 full-sized pitches, it's ideal if you like watching amateur football.

Station Road, Waltham Abbey, EN9 1FJ
Nearest station: Waltham Cross
tfl.gov.uk/modes/walking/lea-valley

50

HAMPSTEAD CIRCULAR WALK

Romantic ramble through beautiful heathland

This 4 km walk will quickly show you why Hampstead Heath has long been considered the most romantic green space in the city. The favoured strolling spot of artistic greats from John Keats and Virginia Woolf to Harry Styles, you'll find plenty to keep you entertained as you wander. Highlights include the stately Fenton House, an observatory that's open to the public when the skies are clear, Keats House, Ernö Goldfinger's modernist home and various ponds where soggy swimmers can be seen emerging in summer (no.48). It's a full loop, starting and ending at Hampstead underground station, allowing you to finish with a visit to the nearby Heath Street Bakehouse for freshly made pastries.

Hampstead High Street, NW3 1QG
Nearest station: Hampstead
nationaltrust.org.uk/visit/london/fenton-house-and-garden/hampstead-circular-walk

51

PARKLAND WALK

Wildlife-rich abandoned railway line

This walk offers two things those who live north of the river don't experience often: almost entirely flat surfaces and an abundance of nature. A 5 km path that you can walk, run or cycle, it follows an old railway line that once connected Finsbury Park and Alexandra Palace. Depending on the season, you can spot hedgehogs, foxes and butterfly species. And – because it's London – lots of graffiti art, so there's always something new to see. Look out for the legendary Spriggan sculpture emerging from the railway arches around halfway. It should take about an hour, and it's worth continuing north for 15 minutes to London's self-proclaimed smallest bakery, Astrid, for a sweet treat – best enjoyed on Alexandra Palace hill with enviable views of the city.

Florence Road, N4 3EY
Nearest station: Finsbury Park
parkland-walk.org.uk

52

TERRIBLE FOOTBALL

Tragic tackles, accidental goals and lots of laughs

The biggest worry when signing up for any sport is that everyone there will be better than you. Forget the fear of being the weakest link at Terrible Football, who organise five-a-side sessions for people who are, well, terrible at football – so no one will get annoyed with shambolic defending or balls hoofed halfway across the park. There's no formal training, just a casual kickabout, but it's a great way to build confidence if you haven't played since school. Sessions are held at 10:30am on Saturdays on Clapham Common and 10:30am every Sunday in Regent's Park. It's free and you don't need any kit; just bring both a black and a white t-shirt and sign up online beforehand as they do get booked up.

Regent's Park, NW1 4NR
Nearest station: Regent's Park
Other locations: multiple, see website
meetup.com/terrible-football-in-london

53

HOLLOW ROCKS

Fitness playground meets school gym

Whether you signed up for every sports day event at high school or preferred to hide in the toilets, Hollow Rocks will redefine your idea of P.E. They offer sports-inspired group fitness classes that include exercises like squats and deadlifts combined with basketball and tennis drills. Some attendees take five-a-side football very seriously and are looking to develop skills and strength alongside it, but many have never set foot in a gym before and just want a fun way to exercise. The space couldn't be further from a sweaty school hall, boasting a smoothie bar, cool branding and a cafe. Everyone gets a slice of orange after class, which will make you feel like you've gone to your favourite friend's parents' house after school.

29–31 Essex Road, N1 2SA
Nearest stations: Essex Road, Angel
Other locations: multiple, see website
hollowrocks.com

54

REGENT'S PARK TENNIS COURTS

Perfect your game in an ace london park

Folk have been playing tennis in Regent's Park for over 100 years and it's a tradition you can easily get involved with. There are 12 hard courts open to the public – eight of which are floodlit, which means you can play in the evenings – lined by linden and hornbeam trees, so you're enveloped in greenery. As most people are here for a casual hit-around rather than anything intensely competitive, there are no guttural grunts to disturb the peace, just the meditative thud of balls being rallied back and forth. First time playing? You can hire rackets for a fiver, although if you plan on sticking at it, it's worth buying a cheap one for not much more.

Park Sports, York Bridge, Inner Circle, NW1 4NU
Nearest station: Regent's Park
parksports.co.uk/venues/regents-park

55

TRIYOGA

Mix up your yoga practice

Yoga is more than just sun salutations, and Triyoga is the perfect place to delve deeper into this ancient practice. There are four studios across the city, offering a huge timetable of classes. These include traditional Pilates and vinyasa flow classes, as well as Feldenkrais, which integrates devotional singing and breathwork, and kirtan, a form of meditation centred around chanting. There are also pre- and post-natal classes where you can bring your babies along to crawl around while you enjoy nap time in child's pose. The studios are phone-free, providing an opportunity to disconnect, and most locations have juice bars, offering a space to mindfully wind down before returning to the real world.

57a Jamestown Road, NW1 7DB
Nearest station: Camden Town
Other locations: Chelsea, Ealing, Shoreditch
triyoga.co.uk

56

SĀMYA STUDIOS

Sun salutations in a bright and airy loft

Switching off and leaning into a yoga class feels easy at this calming studio. That's in part down to the space itself, a loft conversion with exposed beams and beautiful hardwood floors that feels light and bright on even the greyest days. The classes are based on the ancient roots of yoga and focus on a traditional flow that includes downward dog, forward fold and child's pose. Moving your body feels more like a spiritual practice than a workout and you can expect to be chanting 'om' without a hint of irony. There are power sessions on offer if you prefer something more fast-paced, but the studio's focus is on mindful movement and that's what it does best.

19a Cobble Lane, N1 1SF
Nearest station: Highbury & Islington
samyastudios.com

57

BOLLYQUEER

Inclusive Bollywood dance

Joyful movement is the aim at Bollyqueer, a Bollywood-inspired dance class that centres queer, trans and gender non-conforming people. This is a safe, empowering space, founded with the aim of actively breaking down stereotypes around gender and sexuality and finding freedom through dance. It's also one of the most fun places to learn Bollywood dancing. They run regular beginner classes across London, where you'll learn a few variations of choreography and choose the one you feel suits you and your body. It's an incredible opportunity to explore Bollywood culture in an inclusive environment and you'll get a great work-out at the same time.

Old Diorama Arts Centre, Regent's Place,
201 Drummond Street, NW1 3FE
Nearest station: Warren Street
bollyqueer.com

58

ROLLER NATION

Retro roller skating

Transport yourself to a '70s roller disco and skate yourself fit at London's only roller rink. If cringe club music and watching people fall over sparks joy, you'll love their Roller Boogie event on Friday nights. And yes, this *definitely* counts as a workout. You'll break a serious sweat, as balancing on two wheels requires a whole lot of core strength. The bar is open until 1am, but if you are planning on skating with a G&T on board, consider taking one of their beginner skating classes earlier in the week first: they'll help you build confidence and impress your mates come Friday night.

117 Bruce Grove, N17 6UR
Nearest station: Bruce Grove
rollernation.com

IMAGE CREDITS

An Opinionated Guide to Active London
First edition

Published in 2025 by Hoxton Mini Press, London
Copyright © Hoxton Mini Press 2025. All rights reserved.

Text by Alice Porter
Editing by Zoë Jellicoe
    and Gaynor Sermon
Production Design by Dom Grant
Production Control by David Brimble
Proofreading by Florence Ward
Editorial support by Richard Enright

With thanks to Matthew Young for
initial series design.

Please note: we recommend checking the
websites listed for each entry before you
visit for the latest information on price,
opening times and pre-booking
requirements.

Thank you to all of the individuals and
institutions who have provided images
and arranged permissions. While every
effort has been made to trace the present
copyright holders we apologise in advance
for any unintentional omission or error,
and would be pleased to insert the
appropriate acknowledgement in any
subsequent edition.

A CIP catalogue record for this book is
available from the British Library.

ISBN: 978-1-914314-90-2

Printed and bound by OZGraf, Poland

Manufacturer: Hoxton Mini Press, 104
Northside Studios, 16–29 Andrews Road,
London E8 4QF, UK
www.hoxtonminipress.com

Represented by: Authorised Rep
Compliance Ltd., Ground Floor, 71 Lower
Baggot Street, Dublin D02 P593, Ireland
www.arccompliance.com

Hoxton Mini Press is an environmen-
tally conscious publisher, committed
to offsetting our carbon footprint.
This book is 100 per cent carbon
compensated, with offset purchased
from Stand For Trees.

Every time you order from our website, we
plant a tree: www.hoxtonminipress.com

Selected opinionated guides in the series:

For more go to www.hoxtonminipress.com

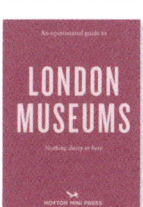

INDEX